MY
emoji™
JOURNAL

Express Yourself
with Your Favorite emoji

RP|KIDS
PHILADELPHIA

Cover and interior design by Jason Kayser
Edited by Adrienne Szpyrka
Typography: Celias

Running Press Book Publishers
2300 Chestnut Street
Philadelphia, PA 19103–4371

Visit us on the web!
www.runningpress.com/rpkids

List the five emoji
that best describe you.

1. Lafe ont Lond
2. Love
3. cool.
4. Scrtthing
5. Pop a moscy

Who was your first crush?

I never ever had a crush because rele late and rele linket

If you could visit any country, which country would you go to and why?

Itly, because it has the Best Pessa.

What makes you feel like a 🦄?

_____

_____

_____

_____

_____

_____

_____

Why is this cat so sad?
Draw what he's thinking about.

Draft a letter here for
someone you love.

_____

_____

_____

_____

_____

_____

_____

_____

What is your favorite thing about winter?

What is the most embarrassing thing you've ever done?

_____

_____

_____

_____

_____

_____

_____

When was the last time
you were in an ✈️?
Where were you going?

Would you rather go diving with    or have a  as a pet?

Go diving wheth wans

When was the
last time you were caught
in the 💧 without
an umbrella?

_____

_____

_____

_____

_____

_____

_____

Who is your favorite villain?

What makes you
really 😡?

_____

_____

_____

_____

If you could ask any
one question and get a true
answer, what question
would you ask?

_____

_____

_____

_____

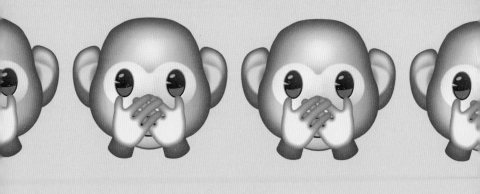

Who is your current crush?

Plan out your dream
road trip. Where
would you go? Who would
you take with you?

_____

_____

_____

_____

_____

_____

_____

When was the last time you 😭?

_____

_____

_____

_____

_____

_____

_____

Would you rather go diving with sharks or bungee jumping?

_____

_____

_____

_____

_____

Who is your closest 👴 friend?

Who is your
closest 👩 friend?

List five things
you really don't like.

1. _____

2. _____

3. _____

4. _____

5. _____

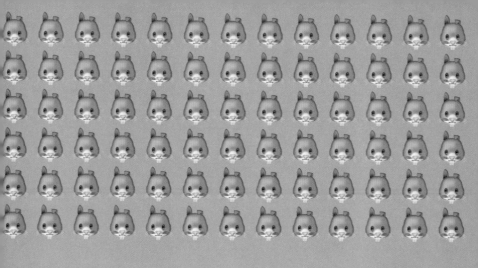

100  or 3 ?

If you were granted three wishes, what would you ask for?

What are the best things about mornings and the worst things about mornings?

What really makes you feel like ?

What is your favorite thing to do outside?

_____

_____

_____

_____

_____

What kinds of things
do you think about
when you walk down the
street alone?

_____

_____

_____

_____

_____

_____

_____

_____

What are your most treasured memories?

Who do you talk to when you're sad?

_____

_____

_____

_____

_____

Do you believe in
ghosts?

Write a secret here that you haven't told anyone before.

_____

_____

_____

_____

_____

_____

_____

_____

What are three things you wish you were better at?

What do you do when no one else is around?

_____

_____

_____

_____

_____

When did you do something nice
for someone, just because?

_____

_____

_____

_____

_____

Do you believe that 👽👽👽 exist? Draw what you imagine an alien would look like.

What is the best birthday you remember?

_____

_____

_____

_____

_____

_____

If you had $100, what would you spend it on?

_____

_____

_____

_____

_____

What makes you a good friend?

Do you believe in love at first sight?

_____

_____

_____

_____

_____

_____

_____

This butterfly is in search of a beautiful flower. Draw one!

If you could ask
for anything for
your birthday, what
would it be?

How do you think your friends would describe you?

_____

_____

_____

_____

_____

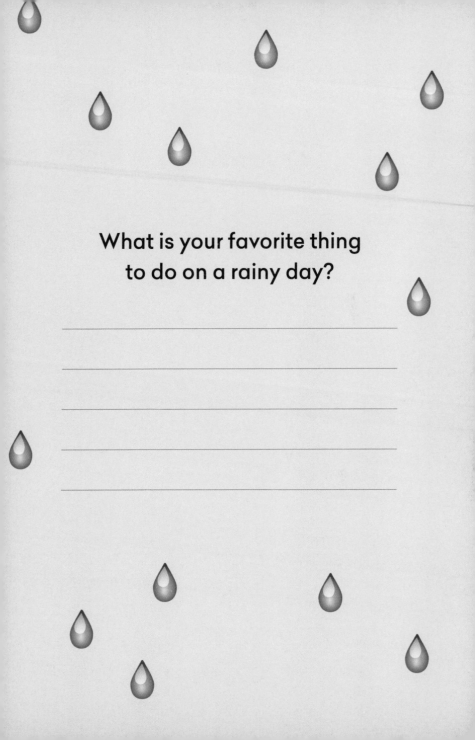

What is your favorite thing to do on a rainy day?

_____

_____

_____

_____

_____

What makes you feel happy?

_____

_____

_____

_____

_____

_____

_____

List five of
your favorite songs.

1. _____

2. _____

3. _____

4. _____

5. _____

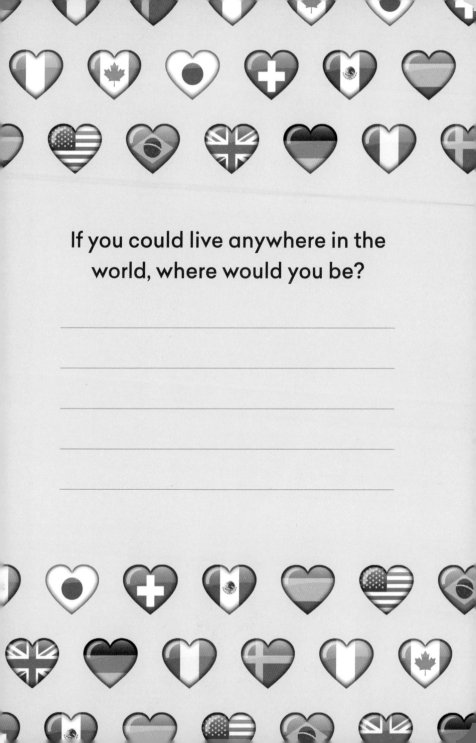

If you could live anywhere in the world, where would you be?

_____

_____

_____

_____

_____

If there was one
thing you could become
really good at,
what would it be?

When was the last time you felt happy?

_____

_____

_____

_____

_____

What would be your perfect day?

_____

_____

_____

_____

_____

_____

_____

_____

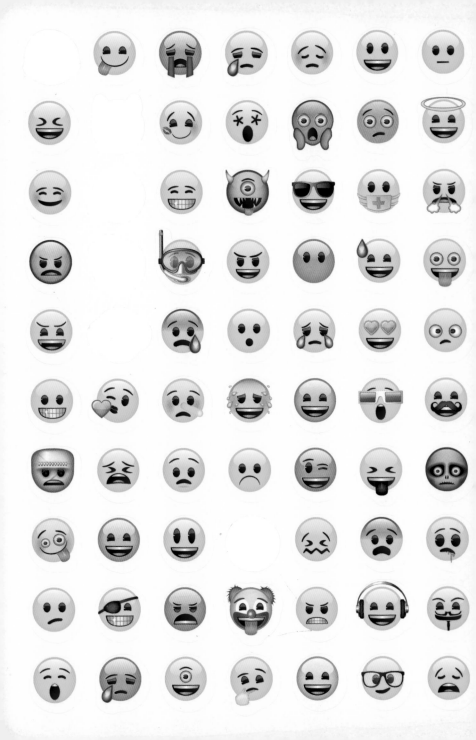

Write the word "hello" in as many languages as you can.

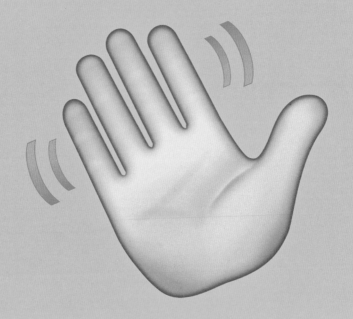

What is your favorite thing to do on the weekend?

_____

_____

_____

_____

_____

What are three things you could do to make the world a better place?

Draw your own emoji.
What emoji have
you never seen before but
wish existed?

What would you do if you won the lottery?

_____

_____

_____

_____

_____

_____

_____

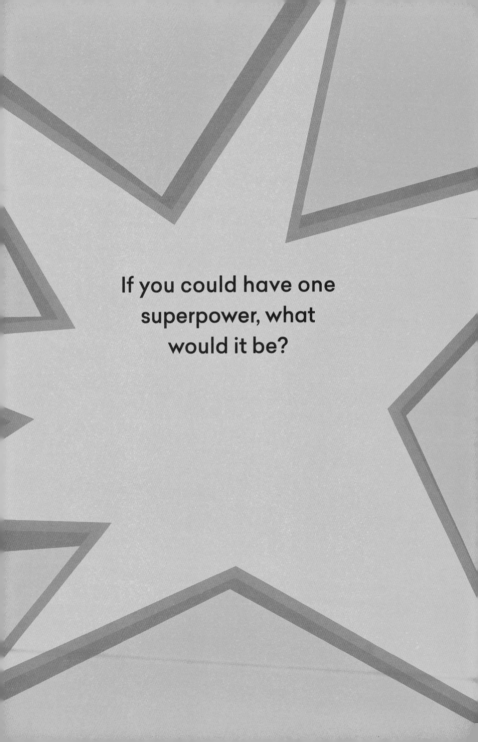

If you could have one
superpower, what
would it be?

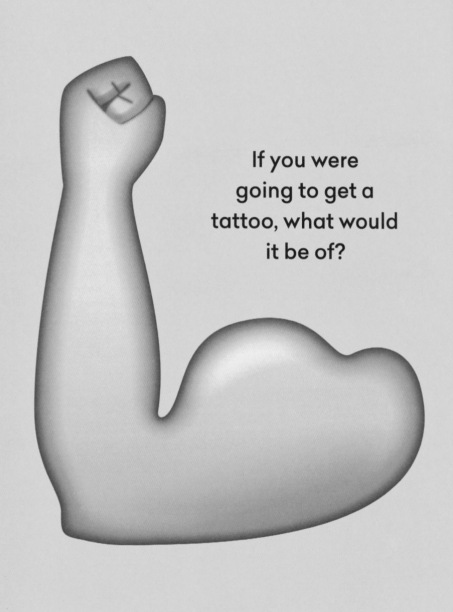

If you were
going to get a
tattoo, what would
it be of?

What are three things that really scare you?

Who was the last person you hugged?

What is your favorite quote?

Is there a smell that sparks a memory for you?

Who do you laugh the most with?

_____

_____

_____

_____

_____

What does "love"
mean to you?

What would you say to your pet if they could understand you?

If you could travel in time, where would you go?

What is your most prized possession?

_____

_____

_____

_____

_____

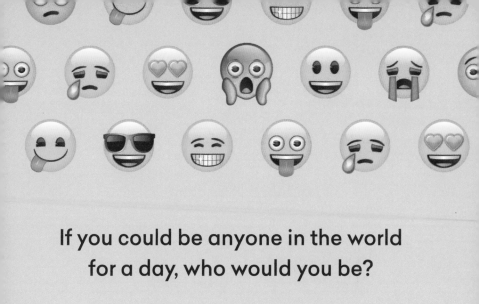

If you could be anyone in the world for a day, who would you be?

_____

_____

_____

_____

What is the funniest joke you've ever heard?

hi My name
is Ginliana
I am in scend
grad I live in
hanover and the

What was the last big mistake you made?

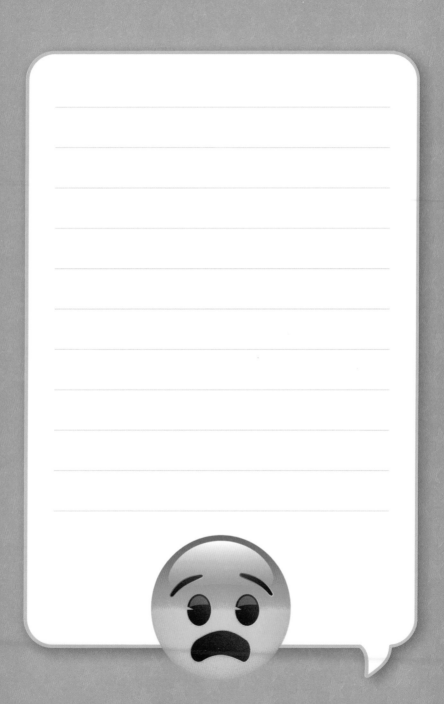

What advice would you give to a younger sibling?

_____

_____

_____

_____

_____

_____

_____

Would you rather be able to breathe under water or fly?

_____

_____

_____

_____

_____

If you could create
a new TV show
about anything at all,
what would it be?

What is the nicest thing you have done for someone?

_____

_____

_____

_____

_____

_____

What is the nicest thing someone has done for you?

_____

_____

_____

_____

_____

_____

_____

How would you describe
yourself to someone new
in one sentence?

_____

_____

_____

_____

_____

Draw an expression on
this blank emoji.

What makes you smile?

Write a funny poem
for someone you know.

_____

_____

_____

_____

_____

_____

_____

_____

What are you most proud of?

_____

_____

_____

_____

_____

What do you think the future will look like?

Do you have a lucky number?
Why is it your lucky number?

_____

_____

_____

_____

_____

What are three things you are really grateful for?

What is something you would like to learn to do?

_____

_____

_____

_____

_____

_____

What is your favorite thing you own?

_____

_____

_____

_____

_____

If you could make one
rule in the world that
everyone would have to follow,
what would it be?

Do you prefer sweet or savory?

What is your biggest worry?

What is hatching from this egg?
Draw it!

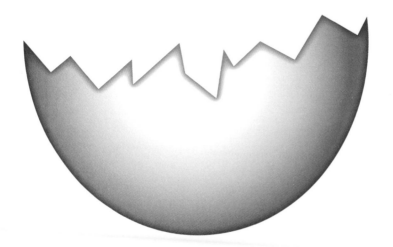

Who are the ten most important people in your life?

When was the last time you got really dressed up?

_____

_____

_____

_____

_____

_____

Would you rather go to the
beach or go camping?

Uh-oh, someone got a bad haircut. Draw the hairdo!

What instrument do you wish you could play?

List your five favorite books.

1. _____

2. _____

3. _____

4. _____

5. _____

This penguin decided to take a trip to the beach. Draw the scene.

What are your favorite pizza toppings?

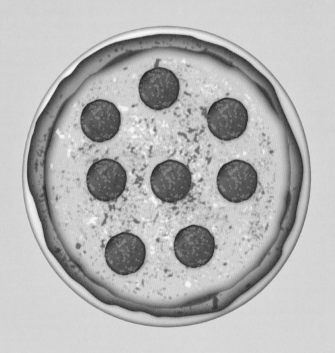

What is your favorite sport to play?

_____

_____

_____

_____

_____

_____

What is your
favorite season?

_____

_____

_____

_____

_____

What do you think about when you're trying to fall asleep at night?

Do you want to draw a snowman?
This one is missing a few parts.

List your five favorite movies.

1. _____

2. _____

3. _____

4. _____

5. _____

If you could invent anything,
what would you invent?

Abracadabra!
Draw something magically
appearing from this hat.

Why is this monkey so happy?
Draw what he's thinking about.